GW00457925

IN THE FOOTSTEPS
OF THE OPIUM EATER

In the Footsteps of the Opium Eater

JOHN ASHBROOK

HARRY CHAMBERS/PETERLOO POETS

First published in 1980
by Harry Chambers/Peterloo Poets
Treovis Farm Cottage, Upton Cross, Liskeard, Cornwall PL14 5BQ

ISBN 0 905291 31 X

Printed in Great Britain by
Latimer Trend & Company Ltd, Plymouth

ACKNOWLEDGEMENTS are due to the editors of the following journals and anthologies in whose pages some of these poems first appeared: *New Poetry 3* (Arts Council, 1977), *Critical Survey, International Who's Who of Poetry Anthology, Phoenix, Poetry Review, Poetry Survey, Poetry Wales, Poet's Yearbook, Silver Spear* (Dublin), *Times Literary Supplement*.

Three poems were previously published in *Death Duties* (Phoenix Pamphlet Poets, 1969). Others have gained awards in the following competitions: Caernarvon Arts Festival, 1978; Critical Quarterly, 1968; Listowel Writers' Week, 1977; Poet's Yearbook; Scottish Open, 1977 and 1978.

Some of these poems have been broadcast on BBC Television.

The cover illustration is a view of Saint Ann's Square, Manchester, in the eighteenth century from the book *Memorials of Manchester Streets* published by Thomas Sutcliffe, Market Place, 1874, taken in turn from *Berry & Casson's Plans of Manchester and Salford*. Thomas De Quincey was baptised in the church depicted here.

The production of this particular volume was made possible by the financial support of North West Arts.

Harry Chambers/Peterloo Poets receives financial assistance from The Arts Council of Great Britain.

CONTENTS

Water

1

As lads of five we'd wander
through the yard and past the midden,

steaming in sunlight, loud with flies,
on hundred-yard adventures to the pit,

to chuck stones, see vivid bile-green moss
retreat in perfect circles like full moons.

2

We collected tadpoles, minnows, newts,
discovered a stream and followed back

to diamond water springing from the earth.
Was it the origin of life we found?

3

At twelve, our first long journeys
on bikes to the canal; we'd swim, taking care

our mouths stayed clear, afterwards
picked off each tiny blood-filled sucker.

4

Pits are condemned as unhygienic now.
Streams have been cleared of weed;

fields irrigated scientifically for economic yield.
Piped water has no magic.

Fire

My cousin had great dreams
of making money,
then reclining at his ease.

He loved the land
and animals,
most of all: cash in his hand.

So, one Saturday,
he planned
to burn the nettles and stray

harsh brambles and thorns
that cursed the ground
beyond his father's barn,

to raise cabbages, carrots,
lettuces.
He quashed all doubts,

set to work with a scythe,
grew tired,
and thought of fire.

It would not catch at first,
but merely sizzled.
A can of petrol burst

it into flame and soon
the scrub was hot
as a coke furnace.

We thrashed with sticks,
then ran for water
but the wind grew brisk,

threw the flames
ten yards
until the tar between the boards

began to melt and then
to glow
with tiny buds of flame,

till half the barn
was bright with fire.
The bales began to burn.

My uncle ran from a distant field,
and we, fearing him
more than fire, escaped to the wood

and hid, watched
flames fill the air,
all the barn burning.

That day we hid
in fear
while we were hunted,

not knowing the terror
we caused, and they
scraped among the rubble

expecting to find
our bodies
wracked and burned.

At dusk they caught us
and having believed
us dead, did not punish

that day or the next.
But before the ashes
had stopped smoking in the yard

we had begun to pay for our sins.

Grandma Scott, 1941

Still she awoke at dawn; we heard
clogged feet on cobbles as she stormed the yard;
from full buckets she fed her animals,
then returned, loud as a wild colt,
with buckets empty a full two inches taller.

Those hard, Victorian hands, like blue pale X-rays,
scrubbed, wrung clothes, cleared grates,
polished the two hundred-year-old kitchen
till it shone, plucked still warm chickens,
to feed mouths of brothers, sons and grandsons.

Almost eighty, deaf when it pleased her,
blind when it pleased her, she neither
heard, nor saw, planes overhead,
could ignore news from abroad,
however bad, however hard it blasted.

The world around her in ruin
she maintained the grim fine cycle of her life.

Convoy

Weeks in New York with 'engine-trouble'
storming the town as all good sailors should
a hundred merchant seamen, rabble to most,
but these vulnerable boys are returned by cops, like brothers.
This tough town absorbs my men
as a ship's hold takes on vermin.
When the ship's ready, they're ready.
The girls are whores, used to cash and sex,
and back home we've families in hardship.
Our neat prows cut Atlantic waters grey as cold dust.
Food for folks back home, everything ship-shape.

I lie on my bunk, shivering, nursing my fear,
smoking too many cigarettes,
holding myself inside my body
while the men seem calm, oblivious of danger.
Afraid to drink, I prop a whiskey bottle,
empty, in view above my bunk,
place one in the washbowl as if to keep it cool.
All this is fraud:
if I get the shakes again
I'll bathe my beard
and act the drunken captain.

I'll see my daughter soon.
Only a frigate and two merchant men lost to date.
Our first flash of land will be a city burning.
My flesh seems to have died.
My thighs are like meat;
my eyes in the mirror above my bunk are blank
as if the glass has misted
and will not wipe clear.
I imagine
the empty, silent arch of a church
but have not prayed since boyhood.

Hitler is a god, but I am bored by visions.
All is reality. The future gets smaller
as it comes nearer.
War hardens me.
I am a pacifist who dreams of killing.
I see Germany as a corpse, long-dead, almost skeletal,
The hand still grasping the scabbard of a mighty sword.
Bombs bigger than warships.
A foetal madness grasps me.
I will see my daughter for the first time.
But I cannot love.

The Blind Man

He left in nineteen-forty-nine;
we missed his fool's grin at the gate,
the neatness of his house, the clear note
of the well when we dropped stones.

He'd lived alone the twenty years
since his wife had died, had survived war
and his blindness, making clear
pathways from each place to the other,
writing perfect letters with a dip-in pen.

The Welfare State saved him;
they put him in a home,
where, away from the familiar life,
the always recognised footsteps in the lane
he began to miss his long-dead wife,
and packed his bags for heaven.

Flesh

We understood it early, sex.
Perhaps Freud is right, we love our mothers,
The world is ruled by the Oedipus complex.
I was six when I first met my father,
He'd returned from war and I asked:
'Who's that man in your bed?'
Got no answer but laughter, then
Kicked out, felt the hard edge of his shin.

At eight we first saw action, ran into a field
And fell on them, gaining strange notions.
They seemed not to notice and my mind said:
'Is that what love is, complete absorption?'
Next time we carried eggs, still warm,
Were about to blow them (without sense of harm),
They were on a hillock, he'd exposed her,
Lay on, rammed like a bulldozer.

We read the books, studied the illustrations,
Saw what insides looked like, learnt
Details of lurid sexual conditions,
What should go where, and what shouldn't;
Visited Blackpool's Museum of Sex,
Saw modelled pricks, dire warnings in wax,
Showing random attachments cause devastation,
The price paid for frequent masturbation.

We weren't put off, still felt the natural impulse,
(Though getting an ugly piece was worse than nothing,
We always controlled passion for sake of status.)
Now, sex is taught, the children learning
Of love, marriage, respect for others,
How boys become fathers, girls mothers,
With colour charts, visual aids on contraception,
Hints on attaining an immaculate conception.

Friends from Childhood

1

I loved that little boy. His accent
so strong that what he said meant
nothing. Our friendship was frowned upon.
This was war. The family were hated:
Hated because they were Germans.
Hated because they were Jews.

2

He lacked front teeth.
I almost lost mine
trying to jump his gate.
His father was a fireman,
all their carpets fire-hoses,
slit and joined, slit and joined.

3

I don't remember him at all,
just his house down a rocky hill.

I know he hung on the tail of a truck
and the truck reversed and broke his back.

That was the end of little Paul.
But I don't remember him at all.

4

A neat little boy, so very prim.
I hate to think what happened to him.

5

Seeing him in the street, strutting, bearded and massive,
a wrestler billed as 'The Mighty Kong'
I tell people 'I fought him once and won.'

Thirty years ago in the playground of Chorlton Park School
I fought him for over an hour,
believing the roar of the crowd was thunder.
Only the bell summoning us to afternoon arts and crafts saved him;
made him what he is?

6

Plump and revolting, his parents rich,
they owned a firm with eleven branches,
possessed Encyclopaedia Britannica,
pristine, never read.
How could I be his friend?
How could anyone like him, except his mother,
his grown, female double?
They were sophisticated,
aged eight, he called her 'Princess'.

7

Enemy more than friend, I would
take circuitous routes home
to avoid him. He wore black,
owned a flowing cloak.
At last we fought. I lost a tooth,
but won, cementing friendship.

8

Big-mouthed and humorous,
he played the violin, scraper not genius,
claimed to be to music
what Hitler was to unifying Europe:
sincere but lacking subtlety.
He brought out the worst in people with his wit.

18

Dullest boy in the dullest class,
daily informed of this
by all around him. He resented
nothing, knew his place, studied
Stanislawsky, inclined to the methodist
viewpoint, wore leather and denim,
practised muttering; communication by twitches.

Fifties

Twenty years since I left school,
long enough to marry and raise children,
make a muck of a couple of careers.
We thought ourselves the first generation
to fight the grim battle of age and class;
admired Bill Haley, with a kiss-curl
and a savage beat,
despised our masters who were effete
and liked Beethoven, or beefy,
keen on games and showerbaths.
We were out for laughs.

They remembered war and many had fought
to keep us safe (they thought)
from Hitler, then the Commies.
We'd suffered war just as badly
and hoped to forget.
It was their moment of glory.
We grew long hair, narrowed our trousers,
they talked of the need for discipline and order.
We went for the spontaneity of jazz,
belief in the latest craze.

At fifteen my first talk with the head,
I was 'the boy whose father is dead'.
He poised his long fingers,
stared at the ceiling to mutter
about God's tender mercy,
offer his sympathy.
But I was an atheist from birth,
hard set against
the acceptance of rules and forms,
belief without logic or proof.
For me dead was dead.

Soon after the same man
chucked me out, for no good reason,
claimed I was an influence on
younger boys and lacked ambition,
said I should be sent to sea,
the very last resort,
this the worst of insults to my mother
proud of my father's naval career.
Thus my childhood, a sublime failure,
schooled me well in anarchy
with fame, infamy, futile glory.

In the Footsteps of the Opium Eater

My father died the spring I was sixteen;
first experience of adult life, first funeral.
I left school to work as office boy, found
this couldn't bring the freedom I desperately desired,
suffered it a year, ran away
to wander through Wales, living on food
pulled from the earth, washed clean in streams,
raw eggs I'd only learnt you could eat
seeing my father, on poor medical advice,
thrusting whole yolks down his gullet.

For months I talked only to sheep,
then worked in a restaurant, quite speechless;
like some small bird ate my full weight daily.
Told to get out I turned without flinching,
let drop the loaded plates I was carrying;
tramped dusty roads, till one bright day
I reached a seaside town, tried to find work.
'We've no need of someone like you,' Chef told me,
saw myself a ragged-figure, bullet-eyed, hairy,
many times reflected in acres of shining plate.

The road on; cliffs above the sea.
I swam shoreward on Atlantic breakers,
crashed onto the body of a man.
They said I'd risked my life trying to save his,
offered five pounds, which I thought generous,
only later wondering how worthless our lives are,
was forced to make sense of my own.
Obsessed with death, I still believe
life may have some meaning
if only we live long enough to find it.

Salford Child

'He was not dropped in good-for-lambing weather,
He took no suck when shook buds sung together,
But he is come in cold-as-workhouse weather
    Poor as a Salford Child.'

John Short: *A Caro*

We knew nothing of his secret pleasures then;
in school he was ignored:
the mildest attention made him stutter.

He disappeared. Inquiries revealed
he'd fallen while hunting squeakers,
his friends described his wild descending cry,
arms whirling like propeller-blades to gain balance,
the thud of his body.

His skull was broken.

Slowly he recovered life,
was seen in Regent's Park,
a small square, the only grass for miles,
in the company of old men
who sat, and spat, and waited to die.

He developed his own quiet, passionate love of the free life;
escaped school's boredom,
indoctrination in his own inferiority,
began to breed pigeons
and to race them.

He loved their bodies' peaceful softness,
their bright bird eyes,
marvelled at their whirling passage
through steel-grey skies.

They were dependable;
they came back always,
returned to him,
who was their own still centre.

A Child's Day Out

A boy, new from the West Indies,
has run out of school, taking
a friend in support of racial unity.

I am sent to find them. The fog
meanders along the street
in front of me. My feet sound on the pavement

as voices from another land.
In the gutter two children
are playing with a long-dead cat, its entrails

displayed by a passing car. Seen
two boys? I ask, but they are
too young to speak. The launderette is a warm

bright haven. We ain't seen no black
bastards, says a white woman
kindly. At the house a sleepy negro knows

nothing of the child since morning;
a woman's voice, his eyes shine
in the dusky corridor and he's gone.

An hour later, in the dark and
mist of early afternoon
Moss Side, I find them, crouched by a wall, crying.

When one kicks out the other grips
my arm. You pinky bastard
he mutters; the tears jewels on his dark face.

War

Asked to paint anything
the girls paint houses, secure,
symmetrical as faces,
two eyes for windows,
the mouth an ever-open door.
But, twenty years after
the boys still paint war.

A war of gleaming Spitfires
and their glory in the clouds
and spinning, fire-torn Nazi planes
and Germans dressed like clowns.

But that's not the war I was born to.
Signposts pointing nowhere,
clocks turned towards heaven,
fear round every corner.

War is memory of what I never knew,
a bomb dropped nearby,
a window shattered on my cot;
and 'father' was like 'god',
a word, but not a being.

Asked to paint a war,
I paint a woman's face, screaming.

The Perfect Freudian Specimen

Angelic, with a head of curls, a bright
twelve-year-old, severely regressed,
revelling in lavatorial jokes and anal
phantasies; writing poems with titles like:
'The History of a Turd, Its Joys and Pleasures'.
The anal-masochistic stage they call it.

But he's led a quiet life, stable
family, the father a gentle man,
the mother respectable, but not unpleasant.
I question her carefully, keen to know
if he's suffered pain from accident or illness.
Yes: he's a diabetic, had injections as a baby.

Thus he received a daily irrational
dose of pain from those he was closest to,
those he might have loved, those
who loved him, though he never knew it.

The Spastic Child

Those thin twisted legs
Spell out, in turn, each letter
Of the alpha-bet.

A Phantasy

This plump boy, simple, scared of everything,
told me he'd like to live in a cardboard box
with eye-holes, ear-holes, air-holes.

After years of treatment he'd reached the point
where only one fear remained: drowning,
nightmares of being sucked into the waves.

In the dead centre of England, walking
to school along a road two miles from any
water, a grain truck passed him

on a tight corner, spilled its load
over him. The driver saw the grain
moving, tried to dig down.

There were sounds too. Long bleating
cries. He thought it was a sheep
he'd buried. Thus the boy died.

Catharsis

'Suicide by the knife, so popular
in Ancient Rome, is rare
in Britain of the sixties
where drugs are superseding gas.

Suicide, we find, has fashions,
fascinating local and cultural variations.
Swedes die alone in the snow. They like to suffer.
The extravert French prefer the Eiffel Tower.

Suicide provides half the patients here.
It is a middle-class disease.
The poor always believe things may get better.
The rich quickly reach the end of their tether.

Suicide, or other controversial matters,
should not be mentioned on the wards.
Look at things rather than people,
ask about food or pay, not fundamentals.'

The patients, seated round a table,
look stunned rather than mad,
like models at a waxworks.

A lady with pearls, scratches, quietly cackles,
a vicar prays after each completed task—
making paper hats for Christmas crackers.

Finally the star patient, knife-suicide,
gaining catharsis wielding a guillotine with manic power,
confident, friendly, keen to chat.

They think she's cured.
But when she tempts us closer,
we see her eyes are mad.

Humanity

Sometimes, seeing them queue
in the corridor outside my room
I wonder if they're human:
a line of suffering women
wearing what can hardly be called clothes;
their kids alive and stinking.

Once in the room they gradually defreeze,
attain recognisable human form.
We try to reach out towards each other
across the gulf. And even I, sometimes,
become human.

Strange Meeting

I've not met him, know his children
well. For years they've moaned

of cruelty, beatings. He locks
them up for hours, laughs at

everything they do. He's as expected:
a bullet-headed Pole, foul-tempered,

bitter, almost paranoid. 'Not English,'
he says, 'That's why my children push

me on one side like a dirty boot. That's why
I can't get a job, settle down or try

to start a business. Sod Socialists. Sod
politics. You know what the Germans did?'

'I know war,' I say, 'I'm well aware
war kills, war destroys, war . . .'

'See this.' He pulls off his shirt,
exposes a wound from waist

to hair-line, flesh like jelly,
the shoulder-blade cut out. 'Fucking Jerry.

I hate the modern world. Russians. Yanks.
War! Bring in the tanks,

smash the lot. Tear up this
civilisation by the roots. It's piss.

They say I'm lucky. I stayed alive,
had children. I hate you bastards. I've

suffered more from English snobbery
than in the prison camps of Germany.'

I sink to hopelessness. The man's
not as mad as I expected; he's sane as

you or I. He's lived here thirty years.
And still he hates us.

The Revolutionary

He's late to the clinic, quite obviously
been drinking; unshaven, handsome,
but put together badly,
or falling apart.
He's brought the boy, bright-cheeked,
squinting. Not *his* boy:
he married a woman with three children,
kept them when she died.

'Girls'll do t'housework but the lad's no use.
I earn more not working.
Work'd be daft. Not fair on the kids.
I stay in bed late with a pot of tea,
have a bit of peace when they've gone,
wander down to the pub about eleven,
get back early, before the children,
light a fire, try to keep cheerful,

in the evenings write articles
about the Spanish Civil War.
I jumped ship in thirty-six,
said to be the youngest recruit;
killed three men before I was seventeen,
and had my thumb blown off.'
He shows me his hand:
'Now isn't that unique.'

While I talk to the boy,
(he kicked a girl, flooded lavatories,
hid on a roof till they fetched the police,)
he studies my bookshelves.
'I read Jane Austen,' he says,
sneering, writhing, ironic;
'No. Not for relaxation,
but to stoke the furnace of my hate.'

Home

'Dear Doctor, can you come to see me.
My chest is bad. My shoes leak.
I've not been out for a week.

Mark is acting queer again.
He went berserk when the school board come.
My nerves are gone, head beats like a drum.'

She's not left the house for five years;
Since her husband quit.
She married twice, both drunks, both Irishmen,
Smooth talkers, cheerful,
Who took to crime, then ran.

'Jennifer got pregnant (you remember her,
The one with a pot eye,
Though she was pretty once,
Till the chip-pan set her on fire.)

Her bloke's left now (I knew he would.)
Another kid to feed. I'm the old woman lived in a shoe.
What'll I do? What'll I do?'

She believes she works all day,
Worn out by cares,
That no one ever had such children;
They never help.
She keeps the curtains drawn for fear of peepers.

'Frances won't come home at night
She plays cards with this old man
Down t' street. I think he's past it.
But you never know. She's indiscreet.

Nigel's got nits. I keep him clean.
It's Pakis at school. They're obscene.
The world is rancid, ain't it, Doctor?
If only I could keep my head above water.'

The house is smelly, crammed
With cats and children.
It's dark and cold, unclean.
The Welfare want to take the kids away,
But they love her, trust her.
This is home. Home is their castle.

The Great Escapist

To Reggie Rubber-Bones Wilson

Fifty, the glory gone, an independent
who buys his own pints,
sits by the bar corner, solitary,
legs twisted three times round each other,
showing the athleticism of a body
still thin as an eel
that allowed him once to scale walls,
manoeuvre bends in twelve-inch pipes,
escape from desperate situations.
Now he's only
someone else's wife to flee from,
drink and memories his solace.
To regulars he's a curse,
his conversation only has one topic:
hatred of the bourgeois ethic,
belief that true democracy
means the end of the state.
To strangers he'll tell of the London gangs,
escapes and escapades,
the body's torture in small spaces.
But it's tame stuff now, that twenty years
have brought to common knowledge.
Like all of us he earns a humble wage.
No longer serialised on the front page,
no longer News of the World.

The Actress

Sunday. We're in the bar for a long session.
She's bright, quiet but still responsive
To others, the perfect actress, stirring imagination,
While underplaying the role. Her provocative
Gaze makes small men grow, until their scruples
Overwhelm them, they turn to face their drinks.
As if a switch is moved in her brain, she crumples.
Her mind behind the suddenly blank
Eyes seems to be struggling with a whirling madness;
She's unaware of bare flesh she exposes.
We walk her home, support the soft carcass.
She manages to speak: 'An actress thrives
Under spotlights. I felt there was a chance
Somebody didn't love me. My body was perfect once.'

Saturday Night at Finches

Breathing's difficult, moving impossible.
At ten I jam myself in the farthest corner,
shall wait here till closing,

the image on my mind one from childhood:
Arthur Mee's encyclopedia,
logs jammed in a Canadian river,

so tightly packed they almost break the bank.
The loud talk.
The lonely, who have spent a week of evenings

alone in dismal rooms in Paddington or Putney
hope to meet a girl; someone they can talk to.
They drink too much, to prove to themselves

they've had a good night out.
We meet a tiny, dapper Scotsman
who insists on singing; a red-faced man,

burly in long overcoat, failed policeman
or pensioned-off overweight rugby player,
bores who will not go away.

We introduce them. But soon it is quite clear:
the lonely do not crave each other.

Men of Business

At fifty they still run around together,
Play at being twenty years younger.

Barmaids, horses, cards their chosen sports.
'Growing up's growing old. Don't change your spots.'

Their talk's of secretaries who'll go down,
Horses that come up trumps, nights on the town.

At home their kids don't starve, their wives
Don't suffer beatings or tormented lives.

Their philosophy is simple: 'Back both ways,
Enjoy life; make sure the other man pays.'

Futuretility

They're taking away reality, the real
streets that hold real people, Victorian buildings
constructed to man's scale.
They are putting up dreams, copies of things
they made in miniature, then multiplied.
The passer-by, not King Kong, but human-sized,
sees only blank walls, feels small, despised.

Blocks must be blocks. The architect,
fashion-slave, has no more choice
than the idiot child in a perfect
playroom. The crowds lose face,
become hungry, mindless. Concrete and cranes,
scaffolding, cash-sewage, municipal blunders,
parked cars, blocked pavements. Dead ends.

Progress

We'll increase your standard of living say the MPs.
More music, more poetry,
everyone reading Shakespeare,
getting excited over the exhibition at the Tate,
arguing Camus versus Jean-Paul Sartre.

But they don't mean that. They mean:
More factories churning out plastic.
More buildings going up, ruining the cities,
dominating the countryside.
More sheep destroying the mountains.
More butter hardening the arteries.
More food than we can ever eat.
More cigarettes to rot our lungs away.
More drink to kill our brain cells.
More roads to split us apart.
More tax inspectors and local councillors.
More social workers and psychologists.
More engineers and specialists.
Fewer people.

The Government Officers

They go to offices in buildings sterile as cancer clinics;
They mount the stairs because this is their only exercise.
They sit on rigid chairs behind desks of mahogany or oak.
They are aware always life may be passing them by.
They shuffle papers, like tomcats making their mark on everything.
They believe that trees are something in a child's picture book.
They believe they are living. They eat, sleep, reproduce themselves.
They have seen the sea and even seen the moon, the stars,
They have seen God in the high arch of the church, but
They have never heard him speak. As their true God
They have Time which they believe is omniscient.
They have feet like puff-balls from too little use.
They have minds like puff-balls, made sterile by too many pricks
   from small nerve needles.
They do not dream but they are by no means mindless.
They read everything closely, searching for errors, for ambiguities.
They have seen only one poem each. The same poem.
They have never been moved to tears except when
They are joined in what they call Holy Matrimony, or
They observe someone put in the ground in what they call Death.
They are clean. They are smart. They are neat. They are in no
   danger of extinction.
They try to be regular. They think about their bowels.
They are not to be pitied. We must assume
They are what they want to be.

The Factory at Night

We work nights, process the sunshine breakfast.
Everything here's run on efficient lines,
We're an essential part of the machines,
And proud of it. Our lives are rolling past,

But we're useful, supporting other lives,
Feeding our wives, our children. Think of us
Gentle reader, stop a moment, poise
Your spoon above your dish. The world's two halves:

The haves and the have-nots. We're part of this,
Man's fight for his survival. We always
Leave at nine, and walk the concrete pathways,
Glad to be a part of morning. Meanwhile,
In rooms that are always airy and cool
Blokes in white work out our obsolescence.

Manchester to Bolton

Between blackened walls beside the railway track
and corrugated iron of Viking's Boiler-Making Yard
two almond trees blossom white tears.

By road there's frontages on view, by rail the back
side of everything's exposed; wrecked cars on land cleared
for rebuilding, left vacant fifteen years,

oil drums, scrap metal, coal-hoppers, slim-waisted
cooling towers. Behind a bridge a disturbed
boy, his face streaked with tears, sleeps

away the day he should have been in school. A raised
pickaxe, delicate as a seagull or a child's drawn bird.
Beyond the Irwell's shining waters a willow also weeps.

The Optimist

To Philip Larkin

Growing old, no wife,
No children, yelling with joy:
'The future's awful.'

Outdated?

'Bonds and gestures pushed to one side,
Like an outdated combine harvester.'
Philip Larkin: 'High Windows'

'Outdated? Can something so modern
be outdated so soon?' I wonder,

then, looking back, realise
it's thirty years since I saw my first

combine (confident, overweight, discordant
as a liner on the Ship Canal viewed

across the flat, potato-sodden fields
of Lancashire) where, only five years

earlier, my uncle had struggled, clay-
footed, tight-armed, behind a thresher

pulled by horses, in full sail.
The years click past. At the end

of a pathway through a countryside of overhanging
trees and scented flowers, the future,

that in youth is infinite and endless, confronts
us suddenly. A brick wall.

Futility

'There must be—perhaps—a larger pattern somewhere in which all these
futilities, these shifting incongruities, are somehow reconciled.'
                                                        William Gerhardie: Futility

I wake at eight, feeling fine
free to lie prone or supine

as the fit takes me. I have
an urge to rise, but no, I suffer

from overwork. On the first day
of a holiday I will say

what I want, do what I want.
I sleep again, wake at eleven,

feeling bad. Two cousins,
unmarried at forty, have phoned,

in a dream, to complain about
my life, my poems, called me a lout,

a moral coward, with no sense
of decency, no ability to face

the realities of life, of making money,
no respect for the traditions of family.

I rise to read 'Futility'
and think of other places I could be,

other lives I could be living. The Trans-Siberian
railway in the midst of Revolution,

Russia, Russia and more Russia,
and, so sublime he's abstract, Uncle Kostia,

who abandons words for pure thought,
believing life's physical futility

demonstrates our spiritual importance;
while outside the plush compartment

to prove that reality is all we know
refugees starve, picturesquely, in snow.

*   *   *

We go out, drive through clouds,
heading downwards, to visit friends.

They're out, and while we wait
I wander, look at a motor-bike, a speed-boat

still sweating from the waves.
And thus seeing other people's lives

I realise they want to speed things
up. My problem's slowing

them down. I'm no movie producer
but a man with a Boer War camera,

hidden beneath the black shade,
viewing life through a damp plate.

Trying to find my own life I study
a blackberry flower, feel the lonely

concentration that precedes a poem,
but receive only the thought that in some

bleak, unthinking lives a rose
can be only a rose.

*   *   *

48

We reach the pub before opening,
and I visit the church, last resting

place for pilgrims, with a roll-call
of the dead. Such walks calm the the atheist soul.

I read the plaque for a dead airman,
think, 'How foolish to risk life,' then yearn

for something worth dying for,
relief from daily boredom.

                    *   *   *

Back home we find the fish I bought
is bad. But she, with foresight,

has bought meat, which I curry, and eat,
despondent in defeat.

We go to bed at ten.
By twelve I am awake again.

I hack at a poem, read 'Futility',
make tea to calm my mind. My

bones ache, I am oppressed
by thought of generations dead.

The day, that began too slowly,
is now refusing to end.

Couples

Nightmare threats of middle-age: everyone I've ever known
meets. Deep in random undergrowth

I am happy with someone I love
but question my future, my motives.

They've all changed while I've
remained the same. Everyone I've ever known is living with

the most unsuitable other person.
The wall-of-death rider has married a one-

eyed man who needs help crossing the road. The queer
fellow who sold men's clothes is having it off with a mountaineer.

There's not much sense in any of it
but they seem content

Even the painter who was wild for kicks
has settled with a county type who rides point to point.

I've planned the future carefully,
used logic. But they're alive, while my

life's a constant garden of spring flowers, daffodils, primroses,
indestructible as plastic, a garden of kept promises,

where nothing new can happen.

Four a.m.

Woken at dead of night
By drips from a gutter that's leaked
For ten years despite
All effort, wet-black,

Jet-black shadows lie
Stark beneath willow
And laurel, and where I
Cleared the ground, hoed

A surface neat as velvet
I sense an absence like an empty
Coffin. A late jet
Roars overhead, I try

To visualise the rows of people,
Just beginning to relax, settling
Back, viewing through portholes,
Their own stubborn emptiness.

Somewhere, something is happening.
Women giving birth;
Love and death. Long
Days of sunshine, the earth

Restoring itself. Somewhere
Happiness is happening. But Russia
Looms like an angry bear.
Japan giggles. China

Spreads endlessly. America
Rolls the dice. Tomorrow
I will solve this problem. The gutter
Mended I will never know

The dark thoughts that stalk the night.

The Old House

No roof, no doors, the windows void of glass,
the beam above the inglenook riddled with woodworm,
sodden by rain. Some modern hand has
added corrugated iron, hardboard to partition a room.

Rubble and boulders litter the floor. Nettles
are growing there now, bindweed and bilberry.
I aim to reduce the house to bare walls,
build up again, return it to the sixteenth century.

Two months of toil make little difference.
A chimney falls. I smash my thumb,
writhe all night, feel helpless.
I think the world's to blame.

* * *

Thus gaining time to contemplate my aim
I ponder the impossibility of going back. We can't reverse
the plod of history. We cannot conquer time.
The world is now; the future rushing past.

I must modernise with water and electricity,
concrete, plastic and glass, send
for plumbers and slaters. Go forward with dignity
towards the world's end.

A Welsh Sunday

Visitors

We are white grubs in the coffin of our car.
We don't like wet fields,
Closed bars, foxy-faced men,
Or the squawking of your women.

The Cat

I leap the boiling red-brown puddles, shelter
By a stricken cart.
I am a tiger not
Constricted by lesser jungles.

The Farmer

We modern men of Wales are not confined
To one steep valley.
My parlour is alive
With girls, and the cowboy's gunsmoke.

The Preacher

My chapel clings like a leech to the hillside,
We have more souls than
Ever. The chapel here
Is alive. Its people dying.

From Trallwyn

From Trallwyn with my daughter,
we follow the lane, still muddy in midsummer,
to the house beside the stream, where
dragonflies fan the still waters,
deep-down brown fish quiver with life.
Across the bridge, in the wheatfield,
she is obsessed by butterflies,
to catch, to keep as pets, to cherish.
In the farmyard a dog barks, then retires
as if drawn by an unseen leash.
Its master, brown and silent as the hills,
stares his Welshman's stare
and nods and disappears.

Through a field of cows, then up,
the slope sudden and steep
to the church in the dip of a hill.
Over the wall she is frightened,
the church is lost, lonely, not used now,
the windows broken, the graves overgrown.
Inside, falling plaster, mouldy benches,
and the roof still beautiful,
still arching towards heaven.
The altar steps are broken, the Bibles
soggy, splitting, and in Welsh.
There is a box for coins,
and a history of the parish to 1847
when the family left for Australia.

Outside again
she sees the devil in a clump of thorns.
Now we are both afraid.

The Graveyard at Laugharne, 1952

He must have known it was coming:
the tree hangs above him
like a great black bird,
grave stones crowd him.
He is fleshier than ever,
flab on chicken bones;
hair receding, fluffy,
eyes sad, mouth sullen.
But above the white full belly of his shirt
his bow is gay as any butterfly.

Tulip

Crimson symmetry

Two rings of butterfly-wing
petals form a cup

Inside that cup a blue-white eye-ring
from which springs
a soft pale tower
guarded by six pillars
of dark, carved stone

Here in an inner world
bathed in pink light
is your Stonehenge

Your own magic circle

Lemons

Acres of sourness
tart yellow and green
yellow-green
green-yellow
among near-black leaves.
Such bitterness
not from rich earth
but the centre
of unknown stones.

I tend each tree
feed rough dung
and pure white powders,
my passion incomprehensible.

At evening cool drinks
bitter as lost love,
fireflies among the trees
as if all existence were
stars against a purple night-sky.

And in the lemon orchard
those tense fruits
like thick-skinned women
a million nipples
round, yellow,
indelicately dangle.

Crash

Stopped while firemen and doctors disentangle
metal and flesh
I watch
a hovering kestrel

thinking this juxtaposition of birds and motorway
must mean
something.
He's expending great energy

on staying in one place, such concentration
among so much
mach-
inery and metal in motion.

He holds his legs extended, claws
read to pounce
on mouse
or vole. He's

using our noise to aid his silence, so our progress
means his.
But we use
others to kill our flesh:

The blood he spills keeps him alive.
The blood we spill
kills us.

Pride

I have been here six mouths;
my room faces south

with a view of Police Station,
Town Hall, Probation

Office.
I suppose

I am waiting for something to happen.
My mind is open.

I fill my days,
while the buses make circles

round me and the grass
grows and is cut, grows

and is cut. Pigeons huddle
under the Town Hall arch, marvel

at the stability of my life,
my ability to survive

such boredom,
while they enjoy the freedom

of three dimensions.
Thus caged, I am the hobby of pigeons.

The Ravens

'Cwark' shout the ravens. 'Cwark, cwark.'
They follow me, threaten me,
Tear at the air with their wings.

Their nest on the quarry ledge is a massive
Mish-mash of twigs, their babies
Large as blackbirds; black dish-rags,
Their mouths enormous.
They could eat a worm whole.

'Cwark' shout the ravens. 'Cwark, cwark'.
They are black as vicars. Black
As doctors. Black as the Gestapo.
They stamp the earth before me,
Attack the earth with their beaks,
Spraying up debris.

Soon their babies are venturing
On the nest edge. Trying their lungs.
Squawking. Trying their wings.

The ravens attack me, drop out of the air,
Screaming, screaming, unzipping the air
Above me, tearing it open
Like a cat on a black velvet curtain.

I retreat in fear; back into my cave.
'Help' I shout, 'Help me.'

'Cwark' comes the echo, 'Cwark, cwark.'

In Flight

Almost evening. I bend behind the slate wall
to hack at nettle roots. Stand
to hear a roar by me,
feel the breathless displacement of air:

a heron descending between the houses,
head forced back, feet and wings
paddling against impetus, against gravity.

I shield my face
but finally he turns, and with slow
self-conscious wingbeats
fills the air with his feathers.

Biographical Note

John Ashbrook was born in Lancashire and has always lived in and around Manchester. He attended Manchester Grammar School, leaving when he was 15. Some years later he went to Manchester University where he obtained a B.Sc. degree in Psychology. After working for five years as a teacher, mainly in Junior schools and with backward children, he went to Nottingham University to take a further degree in Child Psychology, since when he has worked as an educational psychologist. He is married with grown-up children.

Besides writing poems, several of which have won awards in national competitions, he has written both plays and short stories. His stories have appeared in *Arts Council New Stories 4*, *The Guardian* and *Stand* and have been read on BBC Radio. Plays have been produced by the Experimental Theatre Club and Theatre Clwyd and one play won a prize in the 1979 Stroud Festival.
In the Footsteps of the Opium Eater is John Ashbrook's first full collection.